Persian Cats as Pets

Pet Owner's Guide

Persian Cats General Info, Purchasing, Care, Cost, Keeping, Health, Supplies, Food, Breeding and More Included!

By Lolly Brown

Copyrights and Trademarks

All rights reserved. No part of this book may be reproduced or transformed in any form or by any means, graphic, electronic, or mechanical, including photocopying, recording, taping, or by any information storage retrieval system, without the written permission of the author.

This publipupion is Copyright ©2019 NRB Publishing, an imprint. Nevada. All products, graphics, publipupions, software and services mentioned and recommended in this publipupion are protected by trademarks. In such instance, all trademarks & copyright belong to the respective owners. For information consult www.NRBpublishing.com

Disclaimer and Legal Notice

This product is not legal, medical, or accounting advice and should not be interpreted in that manner. You need to do your own due-diligence to determine if the content of this product is right for you. While every attempt has been made to verify the information shared in this publipupion, neither the author, neither publisher, nor the affiliates assume any responsibility for errors, omissions or contrary interpretation of the subject matter herein. Any perceived slights to any specific person(s) or organization(s) are purely unintentional.

We have no control over the nature, content and availability of the web sites listed in this book. The inclusion of any web site links does not necessarily imply a recommendation or endorse the views expressed within them. We take no responsibility for, and will not be liable for, the websites being temporarily unavailable or being removed from the internet.

The accuracy and completeness of information provided herein and opinions stated herein are not guaranteed or warranted to produce any particular results, and the advice and strategies, contained herein may not be suitable for every individual. Neither the author nor the publisher shall be liable for any loss incurred as a consequence of the use and applipupion, directly or indirectly, of any information presented in this work. This publipupion is designed to provide information in regard to the subject matter covered.

Neither the author nor the publisher assume any responsibility for any errors or omissions, nor do they represent or warrant that the ideas, information, actions, plans, suggestions contained in this book is in all cases accurate. It is the reader's responsibility to find advice before putting anything written in this book into practice. The information in this book is not intended to serve as legal, medical, or accounting advice.

Foreword

Pets are great companions in your house, whether you are living alone or with a family. The key to finding the best household pet is looking for the breed or the kind that would fit your personality. A great household companion is the Persian Cat.

A Persian Cat is one of the oldest cat breed in the world. They evoke the image of the rich and powerful history of Turkey and Persia. Aside from this, they have a long, flowing, luxuriant coat that comes in different colors that pairs well with their big, round copper eyes.

This breed boasts to be a popular pet breed since the beginning; it was seen during Queen Victoria's era until now. Although this a beautiful breeds, they are also very intelligent and can adjust well in new homes and during shows! To understand them better, you need to know and spend time in knowing them. Cats have varied needs such as its housing, feeding, grooming, and even show requirements. You need to fulfill these wishes to make their happier.

This book will help you deal with your Persian Cat from the beginning up to its health concern. We wish you will find essential information about the pet that you desire to have.

Table of Contents

Introduction 1

Chapter One: The Royal History and Breed Information 3

    The Legends of the Persian Cat.. 4

        The Beginning.. 5

        Back in Time.. 6

    A Household Cat to a Show Cat 7

        Crossing the Oceans 8

        Helping the Homeless Cats 8

    What the Facts?... 8

        Quick Facts... 11

Chapter Two: Persian Cats as Pets 13

    What Makes It a Great Pet 14

        The Breed's Personality 15

    Should I Get A Persian Cat? 16

    Legal Requirements for Owning A Cat 17

        Registration and Micro-chipping................................ 18

    Traveling With Your Persian Cat.. 18

        Car Traveling 19

        Train Traveling.. 19

        Air Travel 20

    The Financial Matters 20

Kitten Essentials 21

Chapter Three: My First Persian Cat 27

    What to Do Before I Buy a Cat or Kitten? 28

    Cat or Kitten: Which Shall I Choose? 29

    Adoption: An Alternate Solution 30

    Selecting the Responsible Cat Breeder 31

    Ask Your Friend 32

    A Healthy Cat Breed 33

Chapter Four: Creating a Conducive Environment for the Persian Cat 37

    Appropriate Housing 38

    Tips to Keep Your Cat Happy 39

    Kitten-Proof 101 42

Chapter Five: Feeding Your Persian Cat 49

    Feeding Methods 50

    What Should I Know About Cat Feeding? 53

    Pick Out Balanced Food 54

    Dangerous Food for Your Cat 55

Chapter Six: Good Grooming Habits 59

    How Do I Begin? 60

    Brushing 101 60

    Bath Time! 61

Nail Clipping? Anyone?.. 62

Ear Cleaning 101 63

Dental Hygiene... 63

Chapter Seven: Showing Your Persian Cats 65

The Official Breed Standard 66

Training Your Cat for a Show 72

Techniques You Can Use In a Cat Show 73

Chapter Eight: How Do I Breed My Persian Cat? 75

Things I Need to Consider.. 76

Breeding 101... 76

Risks of Breast Feeding 77

Reproductive Maturity.. 78

The Estrus Cycle.. 79

Choosing a Responsible Breeding Program....................... 83

Cat Breeding Process 85

Chapter Nine: Health Concerns for Your Persian Cat.......... 87

Hairballs and Trichobezoars 88

Problems Concerning Face Shape.. 88

    Kidney Problems.. 89

    Eye Diseases... 90

    Heart Disease 91

    Tear Duct Overflow 92

  Chediak - Higashi Syndrome 93

  Congenital Ankyloblepharon 93

  Urinary Tract Stones 94

 Other Problems seen in Persian Cats 95

Persian Cat 101 99

 Persian Cat 101 100

 Glossary of Cat Terms 105

Index 111

Photo Credits 115

References 117

Introduction

The Persian cat is a medium sized cat that is heavily muscular, its massive fur adds to her large size. This breed is an extremely good looking cat. It has a short body but has thick legs paired with thick neck. Aside from this, the Persian cat boasts to have a long, fine, glossy, and lustrous thick coat which you can cuddle for a long time.

This breed is a classic example of a cat, it will be sleeping whenever it can, but will have sudden bursts of energy and will run around the room and play with whatever thing it has. A great thing about the Persian cat is that it will stretch near you, sleep beside you, and be with you whenever she is in the mood. However, she is open to

Introduction

changes and is generally friendly with everyone, whether they are humans or other pets.

The Persian cat is not really energetic, so, it needs to have its nutrition controlled to have a healthy body. You must pay attention to the cat's regular exercise and nutrition. You need to play with it with the aid of toys, balls, catnip mice, and other things to give them their daily exercise.

Another thing that you need to keep in mind is the Persian's coat. You must look after the coat daily, you need to brush and comb the coat to keep the coat from tangling. Aside from this, you also need to clean the face as to keep away the stains on their faces. Although they are called many names in other countries, the Persian cat will surely love you and get your affection immediately. However, if there are advantages, there are also disadvantages to the breed.

You have a lot of things to think about if you want to own a Persian Cat. You need to know about its housing requirement, grooming needs, breeding profile, transportation, and etc. It might be a scary road at first, but we will guide you in every step of the way in your journey with your Persian Cat. Make sure you highlight all the important information to know and learn. Enjoy this crazy ride with the Persian Cat!

Chapter One: The Royal History and Breed Information

The Persian cat boasts to be the glamorous cat in the world. It has a beautiful, long flowing coat that envelops its sweet and calm face. Other than that, it has a serene personality which makes it popular among the cats. However, this cat is high maintenance. You need to have weekly to daily grooming of the fur, toes, and even the skin. Other than this, this breed could get grumpy if not trained well.

The Persian cat has a sweet, gentle face that lightens up when it sees its favourite people. It can communicate well using its expressive eyes and beautiful voice. It loves to be on its human's lap where it could rest for long periods of

Chapter One: The Royal History and Breed Information

time. Other than this, the cat loves to cuddle. However, it is also curious and playful; it will be around new things and investigate until it gets tired.

A different thing about this cat, it does not really like to climb or jump. Instead, it will just post silently on a sofa or chair while playing with its favourite toy. You need to provide a calm, predictable, and serene environment for your cat. However, Persian cats can adapt well to different environments as long their needs are sufficed.

Most people think that Persian cats only come in one color – white. However, this breed comes in numerous and wonderful patterns and colors! There is a lot uncharted territory about this breed, and we must investigate this now.

In this chapter, we will have an overview about our beloved breed. We will give you its in depth background as well as its characteristics which are needed for your initial decision to get a Persian cat. We hope that, by the end of the book, you will buy your own Persian cat and apply your knowledge! Enjoy learning!

The Legends of the Persian Cat

Some legends say that the Persian cat emerges from a mystical cargo, along with priceless jewels and spices during the Eastern Trade. Along with the baskets of myrrh and

Chapter One: The Royal History and Breed Information

frankincense, there were long haired cats that were traded to the European aristocracy. They were known to be here on earth for as early as 1684 B.C., and its origin? Still unknown.

Another legend is that the cat is from a country of flying carpets and magical cars. Then among the fire, stars, and smoke – there emerged the first Persian Cat.

The Beginning

The Persian cat is known to be at least 150 years old. The oldest known Persian cat was identified in mid-1800s.

In this year, the traveling diplomats brought in longhair kittens that were originally from the Middle Eastern countries to their relatives in Europe and England. Initially, they were called based form their country of origin. Persians were from Persia, Angoras from Ankara, and Russians from Russia.

These cats were an instant celebrity in Italy, France, and England. They were in demand and very popular unlike the native cats in the aforementioned countries.

Their long and luxurious hair might be part of their success another positive would be from their gentle nature and their ability to have a great relationship with their humans.

Chapter One: The Royal History and Breed Information
Back in Time

Before the mid - 19th century, the origin of the Persian and other known cats were really not that clear. There were clear evidences that the Persian cat has been domesticated by people around 4000 years in Egypt! There were figures of sleek, short haired cat that were depicted in religious and art artifacts on the walls and some other that were entombed as mummies.

Other historical records showed that the Romans introduced the domesticated breed throughout Europe, which later on travelled to the New World then to Australia.

Some historians believe that this breed is the proud baby of the Pallas Cat and the European Wild Cat. These two breed has denser longer coat that protected them from harsh climates, these breed has introduced the long haired breed for cats. However, some believe that the breed is a genetic mutation due to slow evolution. In whatever version you believe, the long and flowy hair has been a trademark for the Persian Cat.

Chapter One: The Royal History and Breed Information

A Household Cat to a Show Cat

The exact history of the Persian cat will still be unknown in the nearest future, however, most people believe that long haired cat were brought to Europe from the countries in the Eastern part of the world. Americans and Europeans bred these long haired cats and carefully selected the desirable traits.

Cat clubs were formed to record the lineage of these breed. In July 1871, the first ever cat show was held in England, at the Crystal Palace at the heart of London.

Harrison Weir, the father of the Cat Fancy and the one who produced the first and the coming cat shows at the Crystal Palace. He also wrote books which contained drawings of different breeds as well as standard breed characteristics.

Angora was the part of the modern Persian cat. They recognize this bred to have finer, silkier, and longer hair while the original Persian cat were known to have a larger head, heavy bones, pointed ears, and larger, round eyes.

The colors of these long haired cats were red, tabies, blue-cream, bi-colors, calicos, tortoiseshells, silvers, and smoke.

Chapter One: The Royal History and Breed Information

Crossing the Oceans

Mrs. Edwin Brainard imported the first high bred long haired cat to the United State. She brought a black long haired cat, while Mrs. Clinton Locked imported a white cat who she named Wendell. This cat was from Persia.

The first widely attended and successful cat show in the United States was held in Madison Square Garden in New York City which happened in May 1895. There were 176 cats that were brought in by 125 owners.

Helping the Homeless Cats

Breeders focused on taking care of their valuable cats; however, they still did not forget the less fortunate cats. Breeders dedicated their lives to taking care of cat, whether it is sheltered or not.

What the Facts?

There are a lot of wonderful things about our beloved Persian Cats. However, there are distinct characteristics that make the Persian Cats stand out.

Chapter One: The Royal History and Breed Information

They Were Souvenirs

The origin of the breed is truly a mystery. Some folks say that this breed has emerged from the Middle East; however, some people say that these cats are the same with the cats in Western Europe.

Pietro della Valle, an Italian, introduced and discovered the Persian Cat to the Western Europe. He was truly fascinated with the luxuriously looking furred feline. This man was a famous nobleman that journeyed almost throughout the world! He went to the Middle East, India, Holy Land, and Northern Africa. When della Valle went to Persia, he saw the exotic, long haired gray cats which he immediately bought four pairs, which he then brought to Europe. Other travelers, sailor, or merchants also carried this breed from the Middle East to other parts of the Continent.

They Appeared In the First Cat Show

The Persian cat swept London away more than 250 years ago. This beautiful and fluffy breed appeared in the first cat show in the 1871 which happened at the Crystal Palace.

This cat show exhibited different breeds such as the Siamese cats, Manxes, Scottish wild cats, and other known felines. Even though this event happened before the era of

Chapter One: The Royal History and Breed Information

the Internet, this cat show drew more than 20,000. In this show, the Persian won the "Best in Show".

America Loves Persian Cats

In 1895, the United States welcomed the Persian cats in its beloved arms. By 1906, the Cat Fancier's Association was formed in the United States, and this cat was one of the founding cats in the association. At the moment, the Persian cat is one of the most popular cats in the United States.

Famous People Love These Cats

Many famous people have owned this majestic breed. Florence Nightingale had over 60 cats throughout her life. Marilyn Monroe loved a white Persian cat named Mitsuo.

They Are Easy To Take Care

Although they might look aloof and prissy, this breed is considered to be one of the most low-maintenance cat breed that ever existed.

This Breed Has Different Colors and Varieties

The Persian cat boasts to have different colors, sizes, and varieties. Colors are black-and-white, grey, orange,

Chapter One: The Royal History and Breed Information

tortoiseshell, and calico. Sizes of the cat could be teacup, Himalayans, Chinchilla Longhairs.

Quick Facts

Origin: Iran (Persia)

Breed Size: big size

Body Type and Appearance: It has a short body, with thick legs and a short neck. Also, its tail is short and small ears. The head is rounded with large rounded eyes.

Height: 10 -1 5 inches for male, 10 – 14 inches for female

Weight: less than 12 lbs for Male, and eight to 12 lbs for Female

Coat Length: long

Coat Texture: silky

Color: red, black, chocolate, silver, cameo, blue-cream, calico, white, cream, blue, lilac, golden, tortoiseshell, brown, seal

Patterns: tortoiseshell, tricolor/calico, smoke, points, solid, bicolor, tabby, shaded

Temperament: elegant, gentle, graceful, kind, quiet, not particularly shy, need human companionship,

Chapter One: The Royal History and Breed Information

Strangers: not that friendly around strangers

Other Cats: gets along well with other cat

Other Pets: may get along well with other pets if properly socialized, may chase small pets

With Children: Not that great with children, unless the child is gentle and won't cause the cat anxiety.

Exercise Needs: needs daily exercise through running or walking around a fenced yard

Social Needs: Moderate

Health Conditions: this breed develops hereditary health issues. The issues include progressive retinal atrophy (PRA), bladder stones, liver shunts, polycystic kidney disease (PKD), hypertrophic cardiomyopathy (HCM), cystitis (bladder infection)

Lifespan: average 8 to 11 years

These are just some basic information that you need to know about our majestic Persian Cats. We have included its history and breed standards for you knowledge. This information is important if you want to raise your cat on your own.

On the succeeding chapters, we will be talking about how fun it is to take care of a Persian cat. Read on to know more!

Chapter Two: Persian Cats as Pets

We have known that this breed is a majestic creature with a colorful history. However, knowing the history is not the only thing that you need to know about the breed to fully decide if you want to have this breed as a pet. Let us read on to know more about this breed.

Although this cat is a majestic pet, there are still a lot of things that you need to know about them. Just like its behaviour, pros and cons, as well as the legal requirements you need to have to travel with your pet.

In this section, we will be listing down reasons on why you should buy your own Persian cat as well as the things you shall need if you want to keep this cat as your pet. And, we will give you the requirements on how to purchase your cat legally and how to travel with it whether abroad or locally.

What Makes It a Great Pet

Buying a pet is a big decision; you must have fully researched on the breed and its ins and outs. You must know how it behaves, its characteristics, and the care that the cat needs. Persian Cats are lovable creatures, however, they do not do great with pets and children at first – you need to know how to handle this at first.

Persian Cats are majestic creatures that are not really that much of a cat. They like to slouch and will not engage in play easily. They will view you from afar and for you to easily bask at its glory. However, this pet would sit with on your lap, be with you, and sleep on your bet – only if it wants to. All in all, Persian Cats are great household pets that would also great for cat shows. Your friends would envy how pretty this cat looks.

A great way of knowing the pet is through its characteristics. You must know how if the cat's personality matches your personality. You must be in harmony because you will be spending a long time with this pet.

Chapter Two: Persian Cats as Pets

The Breed's Personality

This breed is quiet and gentle cats who want to have a quiet environment and people who will love them fully. This cat loves to rest on your sofa scale your bookcase or anywhere high that it can come to.

This breed does not really like to be dragged by children or be played dressed up with. It gets along with children, only if they will take care of the cat carefully. This cat wants only gentle respect that it needs. Although this cat greets you with a gentle meow, you can be certain that this dog will speak using its eyes. It can usually stand being alone, but your added presence will surely lit its day up.

This breed can easily adapt to any environment, as long as they have a lot of attention and enough personal space. They want human companionship.

Behavioral Characteristics

This breed is a creature of habit. They want to have a secure, stable living environment and do not want changes in its life. It can adapt to different households if you add consistent and gentle reassurance that you will be there with them. They will lounge on the softest place or near their human's shoulder.

Chapter Two: Persian Cats as Pets

Should I Get A Persian Cat?

This portion will give you an idea on why you should get a Persian cat, or not. Look closely at the pros and cons, and decide afterwards if you still want to pursue getting a Persian Cat.

Pros

- Nice natured
- They are very placid
- They can adapt easily, they can cope well with family additions, house moves, and new pets.
- Can be great with other pets, as long as you socialize it properly
- They are great with children, as long as they are gentle
- They are loving and gentle
- They are very confident and playful, but generally calm
- They have melodic, quiet voice
- They are okay to being indoor cats.

Cons

- You need to comb their long hair
- The breed needs to rake a bath to keep the fur in the best conditions

- You need to wipe the eyes daily to remove excess water and stain on the eye
- You need to groom the cat almost daily
- This breed needs help with their personal hygiene
- Although they are fine with being alone, this breed does not do well with belong lonely – they thrive for human attention
- It needs a sitter when you will be gone for long periods of time.

Legal Requirements for Owning A Cat

If you really plan to own a Persian Cat, you may need to license your cat to keep up with certain laws. The law aims not only to protect all animals from cruelty and neglect but also to protect you from the animals from becoming a danger or nuisance aspect to your life. However, if you do not comply with these requirements, you can possibly be fined.

You need to check by your city's rules and regulation about the cat. You may need to have it de - sexed or keep it in your house during wee hours. There may be a certain number of cats that you can own within your household, you need to check to your city council to know more.

You also need to be responsible for your cat's overall

health. You need to provide water, shelter, food, exercise, and visiting the vet for regular check-up.

There are also certain policies that you need to follow, especially if your cat. If you fail to properly take care of your cat, you can be prosecuted and pay fines, jail, or even forever be banned to own an animal.

Registration and Micro-chipping

Registering your cat, as well as micro-chipping, can greatly improve the chance for your cat to be returned if they become lost. When your cat reaches the age of three months, you should have registered your cat with the local council and your registration must be renewed yearly.

Traveling With Your Persian Cat

Cats do not really like to travel; they are usually territorial and feel very vulnerable once they are in other territory. If you really want your cat to be with you in your trip, you need to provide a safe, comfortable, and secure carrier in which your cat will stay in. The cat needs to be confined until the end of the journey, or until the cat has adjusted well in new territory.

Car Traveling

A loose cat in the car is a very dangerous cat. It could cause an accident to you, the pet, or the cat may even escape and become lost.

A good option is investing in a good, strong carrier that is very easy to clean in case your cat wants to pee or poo or become sick during the trip.

There are a lot of choices for the carrier, it could solid plastic, plastic-covered wire mesh, wicker, fibre-glass, or etc. You should not use cardboard or cheap plastic as they are not strong enough for long travels, especially if it becomes wet. Another consideration that you might need to consider is the weather condition of when you are traveling. If it is hot, you need to use a basket in which air could easily flow through. However, if you need to transfer to another mode of transportation, such as an airplane, you need to find a carrier that is suited for the airline.

Train Traveling

If you are traveling via train, you need to have a secure carrier in which your cat can't escape from, but still light enough to be carried.

You need to have a solid base where your cat can pee or poo and not soil the railway carriage. Put absorbent paper and material and keep a spare bedding on hand.

You might be able to keep the cat in the carrier on your lap, but it still depends on the type, space, and the rules and regulation of the train.

Air Travel

If you plan to travel by air with your cat, you need to plan ahead of time. You need to select the airline which will allow you to travel with your pet. Aside from this, you need to ask them how you can transport your cat safely. Most airlines do not allow you to travel with your cat, your pet must travel in the special part of the plane which is pressurized and heated.

It is not advisable to travel with a pregnant cat or a kitten under three months old. Other than that, if you can, choose a direct or nonstop flight for you and your cat; this way your cat will not be disturbed and need to be transferred often.

The Financial Matters

Having a cat is not really all rainbows and butterflies,

most of the time you need to shell out money to spend for your pet. It needs a lot of stuff to satisfy its need and wants.

You need to create a list of these things to estimate how much you will need per month. Some of the expenses are needed only once, while some expense might be needed day by day. However, the price of these things depend the location of the store. Big stores have usually higher prices rather than local stores. And, a quality brand might be pricier than those generic ones.

Kitten Essentials

Having a new kitten is always fun. They love to play around and be active and remain cute. However, there are things that you need, especially if you have purchased a new kitten.

Here are some things that you need to provide for your kitten:

Must – Have #1: Kitten Food

There are lots of kitten food varieties that you can choose from. The prices of these foods vary greatly on what kind of food you will get for your kitten. However, you need to provide enough food for your kitten.

This expense is on-going. You need to find the kitten food that not only will meet your kitten's health requirement, but also within your budget. You can ask your vet for advice and seek help to finding the best kitten food in the area.

Must – Have #2: Food and Water Bowl

You need to provide a sturdy food and water bowl for your cat. There are many types of bowls to choose from. Stainless steel and ceramic are the best choices that you can get. However, do not use food bowls that you use in your house.

You can also put mats under the bowls to avoid spills or messes. Clean the bowl properly so it will last for a long time.

Must – Have #3: Litter Box and Its Accessories

You need to train your kitten to use the litter box. So, you need to make sure you have the litter box in place when you first arrive home with it. Make sure this is already filled with litter, because your cat might have to pee and poo sooner than you think.

There are many available types of litter boxes for your

choosing. You can buy litter trays, covered litter boxes, and some fancy automatic litter boxes.

Must – Have #4: Kitten Bed

You need to provide your cat or kitten with a place of its own. Buy or purchase a warm and soft bed, so your cat can sleep or nap peacefully. Buying the bed before the cat arrives will make it feel special and safe, even though your cat might end up on the sofa or window ledge, it is still best buying this for your pet.

There are a lot of choices to choose from, however, you need to pick one that your kitten will surely enjoy. Make sure to check the quality and price range of your bed.

Must – Have #5: Scratching Post

If you plan to purchase a cat, immediately buy a scratch post. A cat tree will surely save your furniture in the long run. If you have a large house, make sure you have many available scratching post in different areas. You do not want your cat to be tearing up the couches, drapes, or bed on their first few days.

Chapter Two: Persian Cats as Pets

Must – Have #6: Medical Expenses

A cat is a living being, part of this is that they need to be vaccinated and taken care of. You need to give them vaccines and boosters when they reach the right age.

You must find a good veterinarian and ask what are the needed shots and boosters you can give to your cat. Ask also when you need to bring your cat for check-ups.

You need to know how much you need to spend on these things, because it is best to prevent diseases rather than to cure it.

Must – Have #7: Cat Carrier

A cat carrier is essential to your life, as we have discussed in the previous part. Purchase a cat carrier that your cat will surely enjoy, make sure it can sit comfortably, even when it grows up. Add a soft blanket inside the carrier and you are good to go.

Must – Have #8: Toys

Toys are essential to stimulate brain function and exercise for both cats and kittens. Make sure you pick out the toys that do not contain harmful substances or those that are easily broken.

Chapter Two: Persian Cats as Pets

Must – Have #9: Treats

Cats and kittens alike love treats. They make great snacks and reward during training session.

There are many available kinds of treats. It is still best to consult your vet on the kind or brand of treats you need to buy for your pet. Make sure it is yummy and beneficial to your cat, as well as fitting in your budget.

Must – Have #10: Collar

Cats and kittens are not really fan of collars; however, you need to get a collar for them if you want to take them out. This tag is best paired with identification cards that include its name, your name, and your contact information.

These are just some things that you need to prepare before your pet arrives at your home. Make sure you have these things to be ready with any disaster you might have with your pet. This chapter, we have dealt on why you need to own a Persian cat now. Still interested? Read on to know other things about this breed. Not interested? Why not read more and we will convince you why you need to get this pet!

Chapter Two: Persian Cats as Pets

Chapter Three: My First Persian Cat

We have tackled greatly about the history, basic information, and reasons why you should own a Persian cat now. However, our journey does not end here. We have a lot to talk about our precious little feline friend. In this chapter, we will be giving you an insight on what you need to do prior you buying the cat. There are a lot of things to consider or do before you buy your pet. We will also be discussing why it is best to purchase or adopt a cat or kitten. Be open to all these things and understand the pros and cons. Have fun reading and enjoy the wild ride.

Chapter Three: My First Persian Cat

What to Do Before I Buy a Cat or Kitten?

Before you buy a new member in your family, it is very important to know these things or even a guide, to ensure that you will meet the needs of your pet.

Having a cat in your life is a big commitment that you need to do. You need to provide proper care during its lifetime and caring for one will take around 10 to 15 years. There are many cats that are left on the streets because the owner has decided that it can't take care of the cat anymore. So make sure you need to know these things before buying a kitten or cat. Your cat requires:

- Feeding – four to five times a day for kittens, and twice a day for cats
- Water – daily
- Emptying and filling of cat litter – daily
- Grooming – for Persian cats, it should be daily
- Social interaction – daily
- Checking for injury or any illnesses – daily
- Removal of fleas – twice a week
- Worming – monthly for kittens, every three months for older cats

- Vet check-up – as prescribed by your vet

If your cat becomes very ill or has an injury, it will require vet treatment. There are also other things that you do, such as cleaning of wounds, medicines, vet visits, and etc. You also need to find someone to take care of your cat when you are away, or if there is no one to take care of your pet, make sure that you hire a sitter to look after your cat.

Cat or Kitten: Which Shall I Choose?

Many people think that if you buy or adopt a cat, it is best to start with a "clean slate" by choosing a cat, ideally, people also like to see their pet grow. *However, most people do not know that kittens are just like babies.* You need to supervise them daily and make sure to monitor their every move. Other than that, you need to kitten-proof your home, such as the electrical devices and the likes. Further, your *children love* to hug cats and kittens are fragile little creatures. They might end up hurting your pet in the long run. Kittens have high energy, they would spend the nights scaling up wherever it can, it can also meow out loud that could distract you. It could run up and down of the stairs and won't sleep where you put it to be.

Chapter Three: My First Persian Cat

An adult cat, however, is the perfect companion for you and your children. Some cat, with the proper training, can tolerate children and would not injure or scratch them. Older people are not really prepared with the energy level of the kitten and would enjoy the calm and serene attitude of the adult cat. If you get an adult cat, you would now know how it looks like, in terms of size, personality, and appearance. You might be happier if you plan to purchase an adult cat.

Adoption: An Alternate Solution

We, here, will provide you with an alternate solution to purchasing a pet, and that is through adoption. You can either adopt a kitten or an adult cat.

When you adopt a kitten or adult cat, you are saving its life. Many owners neglect their pets once they know that it does not fit their schedule or their lifestyle. More often than not, these animals are left in the shelter.

Although it may be difficult to find the right cat, as some might have behavioral problems or even sick, you can ask the group what the problem is with the animal. A cat with a bad behavior can be easily retrained, and it will owe its life to you. Believe me.

Chapter Three: My First Persian Cat

Selecting the Responsible Cat Breeder

You now have decided that you will welcome a cat or kitten in your heart, and you have made the right decision to choose the Persian cat as your pet. Now, you need to choose where to buy the cat from. Responsible breeders are often hard to find. There are a lot of people who breed cats but will not really assure you great quality or good health.

Here are some things you need to remember when choosing the responsible cat breeder:

The Number of Breeders in the Area

Since the Persian cat is a popular breed, there are many people who breed them. Choose the ones that are closest to your home. Review each breeder through visiting their sites and ensuring that they take care of their cats and litters and if they have good breeding practices.

Check Their Breeder Status

Ask the local council for a list of breeder around your area. Make sure that the person you are contacting is in the list. This certification will give you peace of mind about the standard of the breeder and the safety of the litter.

Chapter Three: My First Persian Cat

Ask Your Friend

You need to ask your friends and family members about their recommendation on the breeder. Aside from this, ask around about the chosen breeder and search for reviews of the people who have bought kitten or cats from them.

You can also ask your vet about their recommendation of breeders or even owners who would want to sell their litter.

Personal Visit

If you think you have everything in place, you need to visit the breeders in person and look for their facilities and see if they keep it clean and tidy.

Make sure that the cat is taken care of, look at their faces for signs of happiness or lethargy. Count the numbers of cats that are there, and make sure they are not too thin or too fat.

Your Breeder Will Ask Questions

A thing about responsible breeders is that they will ask questions about you and your background. Make sure you are able to answer all the questions.

Chapter Three: My First Persian Cat

A breeder who will ask you things is a good sign, because it means that he or she is interested to the person who will take care of his or her kittens or cats.

Do Not Rush

You should never buy immediately after a visit. Make sure you allot a few days before you decide whether to buy from that breeder or not. Also, you may visit other sites to make sure you will get the best cat possible.

A reputable breeder will be okay if you will not buy a cat or kittens immediately, so do not rush to make a purchase or the breeder should not push you to decide immediately. Weigh in on the pros and cons before you decide on things.

A Healthy Cat Breed

If you, now, have chosen the correct breeder it is now time to choose the best one from the bunch. Here are the things for you to check to ensure that our will be getting the healthiest cat possible:

Healthy Body

- Uniform body temperature
- Strong muscles

Chapter Three: My First Persian Cat

- Pink tongue and gums
- The ribs can be felt, but not really protruding
- There should not be any bumps or lumps under the skin
- The teeth should be intact.
- The nails and pads should not be cracked.

Eyes

- Alert, bright, clear eyes
- There is little to no discharge
- No sign of cloudiness

Skin and Coat

- Glossy coat
- Hydrated, elastic skin

These are just some of the characteristics that you need to look out for if you want to select a healthy breed. There are other characteristics, such as the being playful to other members of the litter and socializing properly. Make sure there is no sign of lethargy in any way. We now have discussed the reputable breeder and the healthy breed. We hoped you have made up your mind whether you will buy a

Chapter Three: My First Persian Cat

cat or a kitten. There are a lot of things to learn, so let us move along!

Chapter Three: My First Persian Cat

Chapter Four: Creating a Conducive Environment for the Persian Cat

Persian Cats are majestic house pets. They will stand aloof but would still want to cuddle with you. They can be alone for a period of time, but not really for a long time. They want to be with their humans and cuddle with them. There are things that you need to prepare when your pet comes in your house for the very first time. These things are essential so your cat will have a liveable and happy environment inside your home.

In this chapter, we will be giving you guidelines for your cat to have an appropriate housing, as well as the basics in cat husbandry. Aside from this, we will also be

Chapter Four: Creating a Conducive Environment for Your Persian Cat

tackling some ways and techniques to kitten-proof your home.

Appropriate Housing

Here are the general requirements for housing your cat. In the succeeding portion, we will be dealing with the specific housing requirement for our beloved Persian cat:

Accessibility	• The place is easy to disinfect and clean
Design	• The pet can play around easily without being distracted by other things • The place has suitable location for the food, scratching post, bed, and etc.
Grooming Area	• You need to set-up a specific area for grooming your cat

These are just some of the requirements your house should have in order to have a happy and healthy house for your cat.

Chapter Four: Creating a Conducive Environment for Your Persian Cat

Tips to Keep Your Cat Happy

Cats generally want to stay indoors; however, they get bored easily. You need to provide enough play to stimulate their brain function through toys that would satisfy their instinct.

Tip#1: Start during Their Kitten Years

In order to keep your cat happy indoors, you should start when they are still young. Have a suitable outdoor time as well as indoor time.

Tip#2: Provide Fences

You need to provide a safe screened porch for your cat. The porch will provide safety when your cat is playing outdoors. Aside from this, other animals won't come inside your house easily when you have this porch set up.

Make sure to cat-proof every space in your house, check every escape routes, as well as making sure that toxic plants, dangerous objects, and garden chemicals are out of reach.

Chapter Four: Creating a Conducive Environment for Your Persian Cat

Tip#3: Walk On A Leash?

People think that your cat is not fitted for an outside walk. However, if you live in a peaceful neighborhood, you can walk your cat without any trouble.

You need to start this habit when they are young. Although this might be a difficult task, this can provide the cat's health and your bonding with the cat.

Tip#4: A Place to Hang Out

Provide enough space for your cat to hang out. Install a perch indoors near a window. You can also install a large perch on the apartment patio.

Tip#5: A Cat Condo

Aside from a scratching post, you can buy a cat tree, or just make your own. The cat tree could be shall, or could be high to the ceiling.

A cat condo, or a cat tree, can provide great opportunities for your cat to play and rest. You can also put the cat tree by the window so your cat can view the outside from the inside.

Chapter Four: Creating a Conducive Environment for Your Persian Cat

Tip#6: Enough Play Time

Just like any human, make sure that you provide enough play time with your pet. Aside from this, you need to provide varied activities for your cat to kick, chase, stalk, and pounce. Make sure to supervise your cat during play time.

Tip#7: Bring the Outside Inside

You can buy cat grass so your cat can graze during its free time.

Tip#8: Clean, Clean, Clean!

Make sure to thoroughly clean the house, especially its litter box.

Tip#9: Provide An I. D.

Your cat might not like it, but an I. D. is important for your cat's safety. If you occasionally open the window, your cat will be tempted to go outside. An I. D. will help you retrieve the cat back easily.

Chapter Four: Creating a Conducive Environment for Your Persian Cat

Tip#10: Micro - chipping For Safety

An additional insurance is having your cat micro - chipped. A micro-chip contains your contact information as well as your registry information.

Kitten-Proof 101

If you plan on bringing in a young kitten in your family, you need to kitten-proof your home so your furry friend will not eat, chew, or scratch anything. Here are some tips to kitten proof your home:

1. They Love To Paw and Chew

Kittens can be compared to human babies, they slowly learn about their surroundings using their eyes, hands, and mouths. They are playful animals, whether they are young or old, and will do anything to paw around and play with everything they can found on the ground.

You may think that your house is clean; however, you need to get to the ground and clearly look and see if there are small things your cat can play on. Here are the things to remove behind the shelves and counters:

Chapter Four: Creating a Conducive Environment for Your Persian Cat

- twist ties

- ribbons

- plastic bags

- doll/toy accessories

- erasers

- strings

- hair ties

- rubber bands

- sewing supplies

- small board game pieces

There are other things that your cat might chew and paw, and this includes electrical cords. Make sure to tape down any wires so that they can't be lifted or outside from your cat's reach. You also need to secure your telephone wires, curtain tie-backs, and cords it may seem harmless – but your kitten likes to play with everything!

Chapter Four: Creating a Conducive Environment for Your Persian Cat

2. Remove Plants

House plants are surely pretty inside your house; however, make sure that these plants are not harmful to your kittens. Poinsettia, lilies, philodendron, and mistletoe are toxic houseplants that your cat might get very ill if it comes in contact with.

3. Lids closed, please!

Your cat will always look for water outlets so they can take a sip whenever they want. However, not all water sources are clean. Make sure that your cat does not have access to the bathroom toilet. If you do not keep the lid down, your cat might jump in and drown.

Other places are garbage can, washer, laundry bins, and dryer. You do not want your kitten to be trapped inside and won't escape on its own.

4. Warm Spots Are Not Your Friends

Your kitten will love warm spots on your house; however, you need to keep your cat safe from these areas. Fireplace or wood stove is not a great place for napping. You need to move her from time to time if you see that your cat spends a lot of time from these. If you have electrical heater,

Chapter Four: Creating a Conducive Environment for Your Persian Cat

supervise the heat and make sure that you keep your family safe from overheating.

5. Kitten Proofing

Your cat or kitten will surely love to scratch; you should be worried about the couches, tables, carpeted stairs, and rugs. Also, you need to be in the lookout for curtains, bookshelves, or long tablecloths. You need to provide a cat tree or scratching post, so your cat will have a place on its own.

6. Tell Her What She Can't Have

Our loving cat is always curious; they love to see what is inside these cabinets from time to time. You may need to install childproof locks for any cabinets, especially those that have cleaning supplies, or medicines.

Make sure that the top shelf is very inaccessible. Although this might be a high place, your cat will surely love climbing this. You need to have a place where your cat can't come inside – make sure to always close the door for this room.

Chapter Four: Creating a Conducive Environment for Your Persian Cat

7. Small Spaces

Before closing any spaces, make sure to check the inside of it. Your cat loves to snuggle inside small, dark spaces that will provide them warmth. Check your dryer, screens, or windows. A kitten is naturally curious, so make sure you teach it to be away from these places. If your cat already knows these things, you can lay off with the strictness.

8. Window Screens Are No - No

Your cat loves to snuggle on windowpanes to get natural warmth. Make sure to check the window screens and lock it whenever you can.

9. Provide Enough Toys

Your cat might be bored with staying indoors, make sure you give it enough toys to keep it company.

10. Be Patient

This will be a difficult task, especially with doing all these points, you need to be patient in doing this to make sure you get things right.

Chapter Four: Creating a Conducive Environment for Your Persian Cat

These are just some of the guidelines to kitten-proof your home. We have now welcomed our dear cat in our lives, let us proceed to giving it a happy and healthy home through giving correct nutrition.

Chapter Four: Creating a Conducive Environment for Your Persian Cat

Chapter Five: Feeding Your Persian Cat

Nutrition and feeding are two critical things that you need to address for your pet, Persian Cat. You need to give food to your cat that will surely satisfy your cat, as well as giving it essential nutrients and vitamins to have a healthy body. People have a hard time finding the best food and brand that will satisfy the Persian Cat. You need to be very specific with the food that you will be giving to your pet, as this will determine its weight and energy level in the long run. In this chapter, we will be giving you tips and tricks into feeding your precious Persian Cat.

Chapter Five: Feeding Your Persian Cat

Feeding Methods

"How should I feed my cat?" is one of the hardest questions that you need to answer. Can you see that your cat has a specific feeding habit? Should I be strict with meal times?

In this portion, we will be giving you some feeding methods that you may choose from. We will also be dealing with the advantages and disadvantages of each method.

Meal Feeding

In this method, you will be providing food to the cat only at specific meal times throughout the day. You can give both dry and canned foods.

Advantages:

- You can closely monitor food intake
- You can see if your cat has a change in appetite
- All cats will have equal food access at all times

Disadvantages:

- Cats might ask you for feed in between meals.

Chapter Five: Feeding Your Persian Cat

You can feed your kitten three times a day, while an adult cat one or twice a day. Meal feeding is acceptable to majority of cats.

If you have many cats, it is ideal for them to have their own water and food station, where there is not noise, in which your cat can spend time alone.

Free Feeding

In this option, free feeding is having available food for your cat at all times. However, only dry foods can be fed this way, because wet food should be left out throughout the day. If your cat has some left over dry food in a box, you need to throw it away to maintain the food's freshness.

Advantage: Your cat can eat small meals a day within her own schedule. This is best for busy people, just leave a bowl and your cat will decide when to eat.

Disadvantages:

- Your cat might overeat, which will lead to obesity.
- You may find it difficult to tell if your cat has shifted its appetite.

Chapter Five: Feeding Your Persian Cat

- If you have multiple cats, it is difficult to tell who is eating or not.

Make sure that you only serve enough food per day for each bowl. If you notice that the food is gone, do not fill it again until the next day. This will serve a lesson to your cat to eat in small portion rather than eating it all at once.

Combination Feeding

This is defined as giving canned food as twice daily meal, and giving dry food freely.

Advantages:

- This will allow your cat to eat in multiple, small meals per day on its own schedule.
- You can monitor the appetite when giving the wet food.
- This gives the cat the nutritional benefit of both the wet and dry food.

Disadvantages:

- Can lead to obesity and overeating. You need to measure that food needed throughout the day.

Chapter Five: Feeding Your Persian Cat

- This is not a good option if you have multiple cats.

We have tackled the different feeding methods you can do for your cat. It is still up to you to decide how to feed them. Make sure you consider your time and effort to give the best for your cat. In whatever choice you might have, you still need to measure the food you are giving to your pet. You can ask your vet for guidelines on how to feed your pet.

Also, remember that these are just some guidelines. You still need to adjust the method base on the cat's size, energy level, and health issues. Other than this, you need to give the high-quality food that will provide your cat all the nutrients it needs in its life.

What Should I Know About Cat Feeding?

Cats can show their feelings about their food. They will let you know if they like their food or not. Aside from this, even if your cat gets older, you still need to give them the needed nutrition while maintaining its flavour.

Chapter Five: Feeding Your Persian Cat

Pick Out Balanced Food

You, as a cat owner, should learn how to read cat food labels. You need to find out how much protein and fat is in your food. Oftentimes, dry foods are packed with carbohydrates, which are all right to cats; however, you need to make sure that the cat only gets enough carbs in its diet. Read the statement from the Association of American Feed Control Officials (AAFCO) on its package.

Feeding Frequency

Most cats will eat during morning and evening, so you need to provide food during these times. The amount of food you will give to your cat will depend on the activity, age, and size. On average, you need to give 200 calories a day. You need to ask your vet on how much you need to give for your specific cat.

If you plan to free feed, you need to train your cat not to ask for more throughout the day. If you see that your cat is a picky eater, make sure you switch food every month or so to boost its appetite.

Chapter Five: Feeding Your Persian Cat

Going Green?

Being a vegetarian or vegan might be a good choice for us humans, but not our dear cats. They need to have proteins, vitamins, and minerals that come from meat. However, you should not give raw meat to your cat, wilderness cat may enjoy eating meat, but house cats do not like raw meat. Aside from this, raw meat contains bacteria such as E. coli and salmonella which will make your pet very sick.

Dangerous Food for Your Cat

You need to make sure you give the best cat food to meet the nutritional needs of your cat. You might be tempted to give table food and treats, but these are not alternatives and might be poisonous if not chosen well. Here is some food that you should not give to your cats:

- Onions
- Garlic
- Shallots
- Scallions

Chapter Five: Feeding Your Persian Cat

- Raw Meat
- Bones
- Chocolates
- Caffeinated Drinks
- Alcohol
- Raw Dough
- Milk
- Dairy Products
- Grapes
- Raisins
- Dog Food
- Raw Eggs

These are just some of the foods that you should not give to your cat. These foods might lead to skin and coat problems, or worse, death. So, how would you prevent cats from eating the food from the list? Here's how:

- Store food away from your cat's reach. You need to install cat-proof locks in your cabinets.

Chapter Five: Feeding Your Persian Cat

- Do not let your cat near you especially when eating or cooking.

- Do not feed the cat table scraps.

Advise the people around you not to feed the cat anything.

Chapter Five: Feeding Your Persian Cat

Chapter Six: Good Grooming Habits

Cats are natural neat freaks. If you plan to own a Persian Cat, you need to know that your cat is a self-groomer. All its life, your cat just goes sleep and groom. Even if your cat can groom and take a bath on its own, you still need to help your cat. Persian cats will not just look good when groomed; you can also detect health problems when grooming your cat. Other than this, you can also prevent feline health diseases, such as in their digestive system. In this chapter, we will be giving you tips and tricks into grooming your cat.

Chapter Six: Good Grooming Habits

How Do I Begin?

If you already have a pet, you know that you just do not start grooming your cat easily. However, it may be difficult to start grooming first. You need to slowly accustom your cat into grooming.

Pick out the best time for you and your cat for grooming. Both you and your pet should be contented and relax, probably after eating. Start with short grooming sessions first, then offer treats at the end of the sessions. In time, you can practice the whole process with ease.

Brushing 101

If you regularly brush your cat, you can remove dirt, dead hair and even prevent tangles and mats. A key element in brushing is to keep the direction of the hair, and never against it. Be extra gentle with the chest and belly.

You need to start with a wide-toothed comb to remove any debris present in your cat's coat. Next, use a bristle brush to remove any loose hair. You may need to use a toothbrush to brush your cat's face.

Chapter Six: Good Grooming Habits

Bath Time!

Cats and bath time usually do not mix well. Well, it is a known fact that cats do not really like water. Luckily, your cat does not really need a full body bath. However, you may need to get involved with your cat's grooming – especially when your cat gets something sticky or dirty in its fur.

Bath time can be a fun time for the both of you if you do the following:

- Make sure that the water temperature is just right. It should be warm, not too hot and not too cold.
- Make sure to use a cat shampoo, and that is labelled accordingly.
- Use a tub or sink with a rubber mat underneath it.
- Wet the cat using a spray hose; do not pour water directly on your Persian's head.
- Start with your pet's head then work your way until the tail.
- Use a washcloth to wipe your Persian's face. Plain water is fine to wipe the face. However, if your cat's face is dirty, you need to use a diluted shampoo solution, but be careful around the eyes and ears.

Chapter Six: Good Grooming Habits

- Rinse your pet thoroughly to make sure that the shampoo is rinsed out.

- Pat dry with a large towel.

If you will clip your pet's hand, make sure you do it before bath time.

Nail Clipping? Anyone?

Nail clipping will only be difficult if you only make it difficult. You start the process by making your cat feel comfortable to having her feet handled. Massage the feet on a daily basis. You can do this by massaging your hand along the leg, and then press your thumb on each toe, to cause the claw to extend. After some time, your cat will be used to this daily foot massage.

If your cat is already comfortable in this process, it is a great sign to clip it. You need to use a sharp clipper or nail scissors that are used specifically for cats. Clip only the white tip.

Chapter Six: Good Grooming Habits

Ear Cleaning 101

- Put a small amount of liquid ear cleaner on a clean cotton ball or a piece of gauze.

- Fold the ear gently back and wipe any debris or earwax you can see.

- Lift away any dirt and wax but do not rub the ear. Do not clean the canal as this will only cause infection and trauma.

Dental Hygiene

Your cat needs to have healthy gums as well as clean yet sharp teeth. Any damage to this part could lead to many health risks for our dear pets. However, these could be prevented through regular check-ups and brushing.

How to brush your cat's teeth? Here's how!

- Get your cat used to the idea of having her teeth brushed. Gently massage the gums with your gums or use a cotton swab.

- Put a small amount of cat-formulated toothpaste on the lips, this act will make the cat be used to the taste.

Chapter Six: Good Grooming Habits

- Slowly introduce a toothbrush for your cat, it should be smaller than a human toothbrush, it should have very soft bristles. There are toothbrushes that you can wear over the finger; this will allow you to massage your cat's gums.

- Apply the toothpaste on her teeth.

These are just some of the things you need to remember when grooming your cat. Keep this in mind because you will surely use this knowledge someday.

Chapter Seven: Showing Your Persian Cats

Persians are naturally beautiful. If you want to undertake a new journey of showmanship, there are many things that you need to know and do before, during, and after the show.

Winning is a nice feeling, however, it should not be your main goal in this competition. You need to find a way for you and your cat to enjoy the show. Do not enter the show just to compete, enter the show to enjoy the experience and to know more about the breed.

Chapter Seven: Showing Your Persian Cats

The Official Breed Standard

There are a lot of variations for the Persian Cat. However, the cat federation only conforms to the specific standard.

Read on to see if your cat belongs to the breed standard. However, we will start with the pointing system: Read on to know more:

- HEAD... 30
- BODY TYPE... 20
- COAT.. 10
- BALANCE... 5
- REFINEMENT.. 5
- COLOR... 20
- EYE COLOR... 10

Refinement and balance are the two most important things about this breed, these two constitutes in making the parts to be a harmonious whole. There should not be too much or too little consideration in any aspect or feature of the cat.

Chapter Seven: Showing Your Persian Cats

The 20 points for color will be divided into 10 for markings, and 10 for colors for cats that belong in the tabby division. In the bi-color division, the 20 points for color will be divided for "with white" pattern (10 points) and another 10 points for color.

GENERAL:

- ✓ your Persian cat should look heavily boned
- ✓ well-balanced cat
- ✓ the face has a sweet expression
- ✓ the eyes should have round, soft lines
- ✓ Your cat should contain large round eyes, that is set wide apart
- ✓ Has a large round head that contributes well to its whole look
- ✓ The thick, long coat constitutes to its roundness and overall impression of the cat. It also should soften the lines of the cat

HEAD:

- ✓ The head must be massive and round
- ✓ It should have a great breadth of skull
- ✓ The round face has a round underlying bone structure
- ✓ Thick, short neck that is well set

Chapter Seven: Showing Your Persian Cats

✓ The skull needs to be round and smooth to the touch, it should not be too exaggerated from the forehead, where it begins, and the back of the head, where it stops. It should be as well as the breadth between the cat's ears.

✓ There should be an apparent prominence of eyes and the chin, nose; forehead should be in vertical alignment, especially when viewed in profile.

NOSE:

✓ short
✓ snub,
✓ broad
✓ There should be a "break" that is centered well between the eyes.

CHEEKS:

✓ full
✓ The muzzle should not be too pronounced that should be smoothed nicely on the cheeks

JAWS:

✓ broad and powerful.

Chapter Seven: Showing Your Persian Cats

CHIN:

- ✓ full
- ✓ well-developed
- ✓ firmly rounded
- ✓ looking like it has a perfect bite

EARS:

- ✓ small,
- ✓ round tipped
- ✓ tilted forward,
- ✓ Should not be too open at the base
- ✓ Set far apart,
- ✓ low on the head
- ✓ fitting well into the rounded contour side of the head, which should not distort it.

EYES:

- ✓ brilliant in color,
- ✓ full, large, and round
- ✓ Set level and far apart
- ✓ It should have a sweet expression or appearance to the face.

Chapter Seven: Showing Your Persian Cats

BODY:

- low on the legs
- broad and deep through the chest,
- It should be equally massive from across the shoulders and rump
- It should have well rounded mid-section and leveled back
- The body should have good muscle tone, with no clear evidence of obesity
- Large or medium in size.
- Quality is put to first rather than its Persian Cat's size.

LEGS:

- Short, thick, and strong.
- Forelegs straight.
- Hind legs are straight when you look from it behind

PAWS:

- large
- round
- firm
- The toes are carried close

Chapter Seven: Showing Your Persian Cats

✓ There should be five paws in front, four paws at the back

TAIL:

✓ The tail is short but proportionate in the length of the body
✓ The tail should be carried without a protruding curve and at the angle that is well lower than its back
✓

COAT:

✓ thick and long
✓ It should stand off the cat's body
✓ The coat must have a fine text, glossy, and seemingly full of life.
✓ The coat should be long all over the cat's body including the cat's shoulder
✓ The ruff immense that continues in a deep frill between the front legs.
✓ Ear and toe tufts long.
✓ Brush very full.

DISQUALIFY:

✓ button or locket

- ✓ abnormal or kinked tail
- ✓ incomplete number of paws
- ✓ Any sign of weakness in the hind quarters
- ✓ Any signs of deformity of the cat's spine
- ✓ A deformity in the cat's skull that will result in an asymmetrical face or head
- ✓ Nose that is set on only one side of the centerline of the face
- ✓ Crossed eyes.

Training Your Cat for a Show

A pedigreed cat is best judged for its representation of the ideal characteristics of its breed, which will be held in a cat show. Breeders and fanciers work long hours to get a cat ready to enter a show, and the preparation does not only take overnight – it begins during its kitten stage.

Aside from being in good health and being pleasing to the eyes, a show cat will also be evaluated through its temperament and personality. If you think your cat is fitted to these categories, you now, need to know how to train a cat for a show.

Chapter Seven: Showing Your Persian Cats

Techniques You Can Use In a Cat Show

- Training a dog and a cat are different. Different animals will require different training methods.

- Remember to reward and not reprimand your cat into obtaining a good behaviour for your cat.

- You need to practice the stance with your cat, right from the very start. The judges don't expect your cat to stand erect just like a dog. However, you can still train your cat in maintaining in a sitting or standing positions, even for a few moments.

- Make sure you accomplish all the standards and requirements for your cat's breed before you even consider participating in a cat show. The cat shows will provide you with a lot of booklets to read.

- You can hire an expert to train you and your cat for the cat show. Cat associations will provide you with a mentor program that can provide newcomers in the world of cat shows to be accustomed to the process.

Remember These Things!

If you believe that your cat can enter the show, do not be afraid to enter your cat to a show. Many newcomers walk

Chapter Seven: Showing Your Persian Cats

away with numerous prizes because there are many categories with many awards.

Most people also like the atmosphere in cat shows. However, an unspoken rule is to not enter an indoor or outdoor cat into shows. The reason for this rule is that cats that are allowed to roam freely whenever they like to are more vulnerable to diseases and injuries. Other than these, outside/indoor cats are difficult to good grooming.

These are just some of the things to know if you want to enter your cat into a show. You need to start training your cat at an early age. If you believe that your cat has passed all the breed standards, start right away and trains your cat today!

Chapter Eight: How Do I Breed My Persian Cat?

There will come a time when you want to breed your Persian Cat. If you want to continue your cat's beautiful lineage, better prepare for the breeding days before the event comes. However, if you do not want to continue the lineage of your cat, better have it spayed or neutered at an early age.

Whatever you decide to do with your cat, we will still give you an insight on how to breed your Persian cat in this chapter.

Chapter Eight: How Do I Breed My Persian Cat?

Things I Need to Consider

Cats love to reproduce, they can produce babies whenever they want and to whomever they want. Unneutered male, also known as Tom Cats, will roam very far from their place to find the female to reproduce with. The female in heat will welcome any tom cat wherever and whenever they show up.

In this day and age, you need to be more responsible in keeping your cat, or to spay and neuter our cats to prevent abrupt reproduction.

Reputable breeders are very responsible in finding appropriate home for kittens and older cats. They do not want cats that are found in shelters and rescues.

The cats in shelters were usually from backyard breeders or cats that are fed well but not taken care of, and are not spayed or neutered at an appropriate age.

Breeding 101

When your cat has produced the kittens, you need to breast feed the kittens right away. Breast feeding the kittens ensures that the kittens will receive all the nutritional

Chapter Eight: How Do I Breed My Persian Cat?

requirements. Although there are risks that can occur when the cat breast feeds her kittens, the benefits outweigh the risks.

Could I Give Formula?

Many owners prefer to give their kittens formula instead of breast milk, especially if the breast milk gives the kittens diarrhea. However, some kittens have sensitive digestive system and can't always adjust to formula.

Ask your vet on what to do when this happen.

Risks of Breast Feeding

There is only a low risk of breast feeding, but there will be some occurrence. The highest risk of this task is your cat will have sore or infected nipples. The risk will increase when the kittens will grow older and develop strong teeth and claws.

In other cases, the mom's nipples can be so infected that you need to feed your kitten formula milk. On a very rare case, the mother cat will develop eclampsia. This disorder happens when the calcium level in the cat's blood drops suddenly; it is a life threatening condition that

Chapter Eight: How Do I Breed My Persian Cat?

immediately need vet treatment.

If you know that your cat will have kittens soon, it is best to remember that breast feeding is still the best option. However, you need to keep a keen eye on the cat's nipples for any signs of wounds or infections, and be acquainted with the signs and symptoms of eclampsia.

Reproductive Maturity

Queens, also known as the female cats, vary greatly in age when they first reach their reproductive maturity. Some cats will reach their first heat cycle as early as five or six month of age, while some cats do not reach sexual maturity until they reach the 10 to 12 months of age, or even older.

The full heat cycle, also known as the estrous cycle, will last for as little as four days or as long as 30 days. The average cycle will last for six days. In a typical cat, she will reach puberty at around eight to nine months of age. Long haired cats will start their cycle later than their short haired family.

Chapter Eight: How Do I Breed My Persian Cat?

The Estrus Cycle

There are four phases of the cat's estrus cycle. There is an individual variation of the length in each phase, which could prove to be difficult to determine when your female is ready to conceive. The four stages of the cat's cycle are:

- proestrus
- estrus
- interestrus
- anestrus

The following are the stages, in detail:

Stage 1 (Proestrus)

- First stage of being in heat
- This stage lasts for about one to two days.
- The female cat's vulva will be slightly swollen and be moist.
- Your cat might have an increase in appetite but a bit restless
- Males will be very interested, but she will not reciprocate the feelings

Chapter Eight: How Do I Breed My Persian Cat?

Stage 2 (Estrus)

- Second stage of the female heat's cycle

- This period is when the sexual reproduction occurs, and what we commonly refer to being in 'heat'

- This cycle usually lasts for around four to 10 days

- By this time, you should plan the breeding.

- The female will be different around this time; she will be very affectionate and will rub against all the people in the household.

- She will be very vocal about her feelings.

Stage 3 (Interestrus)

- This third stage will last for one to two weeks.

- During this phase, the queen will not like to mate with male and will reject aggressively if the male attempts to breed her.

- If the female was not bred during the estrus cycle, she will remain in the interestrus cycle for a week or two then starts a new cycle.

- If she was successfully bred but did not conceive successfully, she will have a pseudopregnancy (false pregnancy), which will last for around two months

Chapter Eight: How Do I Breed My Persian Cat?

and can lie even to the most successful breeder.

Stage 4 (Anestrus)

- The fourth stage of the heat cycle
- This is the period when the female reproductive system will be at rest.
- You will also get a rest time.

Sometimes, the female cats are polyestrous, which means that they will have repeated cycles, in these cycles, they can still get pregnant. These cycles are greatly affected by daylight, environmental temperature, and presence of other cats.

When there is more than 12 hours of daylight, the female cat's hormones are triggered and she will go into her heat cycle. Most cats are usually bred in March and September or October to March.

Things You Need to Remember

- The female cat's heat cycle varies due to external factors. This is the phase where the female cat is very receptive to its male counterpart.
- If the female cat is not bred when she is receptive to

Chapter Eight: How Do I Breed My Persian Cat?

its counterpart, the heat phase will only last for as little as two days. However, it may also last as long as 19 days.

- Some female cats never come out of the heat, especially during early Spring. The female cat's hormone levels and the visible signs of heat just wane and wax.

- Female cats needed to be impregnated in order to be pregnant. The physical mating of the two cats is needed for the female cat to ovulate.

- If you have successfully bred the male and female, the heat cycle will shorten because eggs will be released from the ovaries due to the hormone surge of being bred.

- You need to have four successful breeding in order to have ovulation in most female cats.

- If there is only one successful breeding, there is only a 50% chance of ovulation in female cats.

- The ovulation period occurs between 24 to 72 hours after the mating of the two cats.

- There will be minimal signs of heat; some owners may even think that their kitten is ill.

- A female cat in heat will exhibit the following

Chapter Eight: How Do I Breed My Persian Cat?

characteristics: roll over, cry, elevate the rear of its tail and hold it to the side, there will be a spine drop if you pet it on her forequarters.

- The cat would likely be interested in going outside, especially if there are male cats present around the area, and will show increase love for their humans.

Choosing a Responsible Breeding Program

Whatever breeding program you may choose, you still need to accomplish the complete medical check-up between the pairs that you are breeding.

These check-ups include for tests for sexually transmitted diseases, blood tests, and x-rays. The cats that will be involved in the breeding process needs a well-documented medical history as well as the medical history of the siblings and parents. The program you are choosing should give special attention to the genetic background of the pairs.

Responsible breeding programs for cat will not risk your cat's health for the sake of breeding. You should not breed your cat before it reaches two years old, and the cat should only be bred every other year. Breeding programs will put a cap on the number of litters that the cat will

Chapter Eight: How Do I Breed My Persian Cat?

produce; they will also require having medical check-up for the female, before and after breeding litters.

Responsible breeding programs are founded to maintain and preserve the health and quality of cat breeders around the world; these programs should not dwell on the financial gain or marketing purposes. If the breeding program that you have chosen has promised you financial rewards because you have bred the cat, you need to walk away immediately, because they only think about the profit and not the health of the cat.

Your chosen breeding program needs to put out all the financial matters that will happen during the breeding process. Breeding your cat will result to you shelling out money and professional breeders have already set aside money for the breeding exercises.

Before you set your mind on your chosen breeding program, make sure you have researched thoroughly. You can talk to your veterinarian about the best breeding program that fits your cat the best, you may even ask cat clubs and conferences about the breeding program that they can recommend.

Chapter Eight: How Do I Breed My Persian Cat?

Cat Breeding Process

Cats really like to reproduce within their lifetime. Ever since the ancient times, the Egyptians worshiped cat to be the fertility symbol, and the female cat, also called the queen, is associated with fecundity. It is a mere coincidence that female cats are in heat during spring, which falls during Valentine's Day.

Other than this, a recent research, if we allow to naturally mate the male and female cat, the female cat can have two or three litters! It would result to 50 to 150 offspring during the lifetime. We can compare this to the trait for the rabbit, which can have multiple litters.

When the female cat is bred with its male counterpart, ovulation will result. Female cats are "induced ovulators" which means that they need to be stimulated before the eggs ovulate. If, during their heat, there are other male cats present in the area, multiple breeding may occur.

It needs around one to three days before the hormone levels drop, especially during its first breeding. Multiple offspring is a result of having more than one male mate.

The mating process will only continue up to three days, especially when the female cat enters the full heat cycle. It is quite difficult to know whether or not your cat is

Chapter Eight: How Do I Breed My Persian Cat?

pregnant or not. Some female cats will experience false pregnancy or pseudo-pregnancy like dogs, but cats will not really show symptoms.

The normal cat pregnancy occurs around 65 days, though this range is average, and considered normal.

These are the points that you need to remember about breeding your cat. Make sure you have highlighted enough information for when the time comes; you have already made up your mind.

Chapter Nine: Health Concerns for Your Persian Cat

Having pets is not always happiness and rainbows; there will come a time when your cat might experience some sadness – especially when it is sick.

Make sure you are ready when your cat is sick; you need to be strong because your cat is counting on you to take care of it. In this chapter, we will discuss the health concerns about our beloved Persian Cat.

Chapter Nine: Health Concerns for Your Cat

Hairballs and Trichobezoars

Persian Cats are long haired cats. This means, these cats will suffer from problems especially hairballs.

You can decrease this problem by giving your cat quality good food, reducing stress, and regular brushing. Stress and low quality food will contribute to excess shedding and hair loss for the cats.

Cats usually eat their hairballs which would lead to a number of hairballs in the stomach. Your cat would suffer badly and would have a lot of serious health consequences. You need help from your veterinarian to solve this problem.

You need to comb your cat daily and ensure that all the dead hair be removed to prevent trichobezoars and hairballs. If you think your cat is suffering from hairballs, you need to give it some malts or pharmaceutical paraffin oil.

Problems Concerning Face Shape

The trend for Persian cat breeding is cross breeding it with cats with extremely pushed noses, and your cat will suffer because of these.

The more pushed the nose is, the more problems your cat will have. Some problems will include tear ducts that will run and stain the fur below the eyes, if you will not mind this, it will cause sores on the skin.

Hair on the nose and eyelashes will cause problems when your cat brushes or rubs its eyes. Other than this, the short nose will cause breathing problems that would make them vulnerable to problems especially due to warm or cold temperatures. The longer noses could give the air to warm or cool down before it enters the body, in which the Persian cat cannot. Your Persian cat will have small nasal passages and can't take much physical exertion as other cats, and they will be very lazy.

Bad bite, or malocclussions, is also common to Persians. You should check this one before buying or purchasing your kitten. Because of this facial deformity, your cat will have a difficulty in eating.

Due to its distorted head shape, your Persian cat will have difficulty birthing kittens because the kitten's head can't pass easily. Aside from this, your Persian cat could give birth to still born kittens.

Kidney Problems

Polycystic Kidney Disease, or PKD, is one of the major health concerns with Persian cats. More than one third of Persian cats are seen to develop PKD. 38% of cats suffer from this hereditary disease.

Chapter Nine: Health Concerns for Your Cat

There are cysts that grow in their kidney that would possibly lead to kidney failure. This problem is seen for your Persian kittens as young as three years old, but can also be seen with cats at the age of 6.

Excessive drinking is the first sign of the problem for PKD. This is a genetic mutation, so you should not buy purebred kittens from breeders who can't provide you with enough papers showing that the parents do not have PKD.

You should have annual ultrasounds for Persian cats after their one year. Unmonitored cats will suddenly collapse at seven to eight years and would die due to complication of the kidney problems. Immediately call your vet when you found renal cysts in your Persian cat. There are appropriate treatments to alleviate this condition.

Eye Diseases

Due to the special shape of our cat's eyes, it will also lead to certain problems. Some of the common ocular diseases of the Persian cats:

- The Conginetal ankyloblepharon is the inherited abnormality that occurs to blue-eyes Persian Cats. This is the union of the membrane between the upper and lower eyelids.

- Congenital epiphora happens when there is an excessive tearing of the tear duct. This will result to oxidation of the hair around their area, there will be an infection by bacteria or fungi around the affected area. This is an hereditary diseases, and there are specific medications that will alleviate this anomaly.

- When the eyelashes rub and irritate the cat's cornea that will result to inversion of the eyelid edges is what we call Entropion. This will cause excessive tearing, where the cats have narrowed eyes and a corneal valscularisation that will produce ulcerations. This needs surgical treatment.

- In Primary glaucoma, there is an excessive blood pressure in the eye that will result in opacity and vision loss. This will be treated through surgery.

Heart Disease

Less than 10% of Persian cats have Hypertrophic cardiomyopathy that would cause an enlargement of the left heart chamber that will result to sudden death. However, this is only more common in male rather than female cats.

A consequence of the incorrect breathing is your cat having a heart problem. Aside from this, if your cat is obese, it will surely develop this disease.

Chapter Nine: Health Concerns for Your Cat
Tear Duct Overflow

The tear duct overflow will occur at mostly any cats, however, this is more prevalent for our lovely cat breed due to their flat features. The face features will result to failure of tears to drain away properly. There is an overproduction of tears that is caused by infections, some of an irritant and allergies.

Other than this, the form of the Persian cat's face adds a factor to the drainage of the problem due to wrinkling of the drainage ducts, shallow tear lakes on the innermost corner of the eyes, and an abnormally small tear duct openings. This condition is believed to a chronic condition in Ultras due to their breeding techniques.

There are several symptoms to look out for, such as the watery discharge in their eyes, ulceration, and tear straining below the eye as well as obvious signs of irritations of your pet below their eyes.

To fully treat the tear duct overflow, you need ot have antibiotic ointment and it is very important to keep these areas, around the eyes, clean to prevent further infections. You also need to carefully trim the hair beneath the eyes, but do it very carefully; this act will also help the drainage.

Dandelion and German Chamomile are just some of the natural herbal ingredients that are natural eye cleaners; these are very tonic in nature and can be seen to soothe your cat. However, in some serious cases, your cat may need to undergo or require surgery.

Chapter Nine: Health Concerns for Your Cat

Chediak - Higashi Syndrome

The Chediak-Higashi syndrome is a condition that is a common health concern for Persians. This is an autosomal recessive genetic disorder that would cause your pet's hair turn into a smoky blue color. However, the dangerous part of this disease is that the condition is the development of nuclear cataracts that are well associated with it. The infections caused by this disease can cause bleeding in your cat.

If your Persian cat has already this condition, they are very prone to infections. There is no clear treatment for this syndrome, as for now.

The symptoms of this syndrome that you need to be in the lookout for are nerve problem in the cat's leg, muscle weakness, numbness, as well as tremors. In serious cases, your cat might experience seizures and what would follow is your cat's death.

Congenital Ankyloblepharon

This disease is common to the Blue Persian cats. This happens where there is adhesion of the eyelids margin, or when they stick with each other. This is a common condition for both kittens and puppies, but very uncommon to adult cats. However, if this persists, this would result to infections and swelling as well as serious eye condition.

You may use a warm, wet cotton ball to free the cat's eyelids, if this does not do the trick, you may need to rush the cat to your vet for further assistance.

Urinary Tract Stones

All cats have this disease; however, this is more prevalent in Persian cats. The Urinary Tract stones are small stones that are found within your cat's bladder, and in most cases, they are carried with the urine. If the puss up and are not passes, this will become an emergency situation, because this blocks the urinary tract.

Some symptoms of the urinary tract stones are the following: abnormal urine pattern, as well as frequent urinating or even difficulty in urinating. You need also to look out for blood in the urine or even cloudy urine.

Magnesium, ammonium, and phosphate are the primary elements that make up the stones. You may need to shift to a low magnesium diet that will eliminate these stones.

Chapter Nine: Health Concerns for Your Cat

Other Problems seen in Persian Cats

- Some Persian cats develop side effect when ingesting Grisofulvin, a ringworm medication.

- Some Persian cats will have behavior problems and simply stop using their litter box, which would also lead to kidney problems.

- Some might even be prone to hip dysplasia.

- Eye diseases are common in this breed.

- If you do not groom your cat well enough, it will cause hair mats which will be very painful when you remove it to your cat.

- Oculocutaneous albinism is a recessive trait that causes a mild autosomal kind of albinism which affects the cat's fur, making it lighter than normal. The effects of this anomaly are more evident when the cat suffers from photophobia and is more sensitive to infections. The veterinarian should treat the symptoms. Here you can learn all about caring for an albino cat.

- The irritation of the Persian cat's creases due to the excessive tear overflow is what we call Skin fold dermatitis. Make sure to contact your vet immediately when you see this.

Chapter Nine: Health Concerns for Your Cat

- If you see scaly and or greasy skin, probably, your cat has oily seborrhea. Oily seborrhea should only be treated by a vet.

- The lameness in your cat that prevents it from jumping without much force is hesitation is what we call Patellar luxation.

- When the joint between the socket of the hip and top of the femur fails, your cat will experience hip dysplasia. This will cause pain and lameness when your cat is moving.

80% of obese Persian cats suffer from Kidney stones. Fortunately, these stones can be removed easily through surgery.

You need to clearly inspect the litter before you purchase it. You need to find a good breeder that will prove to you that the parents are good quality. Aside from this, the parents should also be tested for genetic health problems.

A concern for the breed is that breeders really like or select the mates with undesirable traits such as extremely pushed nose.

These are the health conditions of our beloved furry Persian cat, you can avoid these situations if you have chosen the correct cat from the start – so be in the look out. Unhealthy or sick cats need special treatments and love and care from you.

Chapter Nine: Health Concerns for Your Cat

The Persian cat is the most docile and gentle cat breed of all the cat breeds. You need to keep this breed indoors to keep them free from any diseases and parasites. They would still make lovely house companions even through their health conditions

Chapter Nine: Health Concerns for Your Cat

Persian Cat 101

We have discussed everything that you need to know about our dearest Persian cat. Now, what to do with that knowledge? Go out and buy your first pet right now! However, there are still a lot of things in about the cat that we have provided. You can look up additional info about the cat in other books or websites. Remember, more knowledge about this breed, the better!

In this final chapter, we will be recapping everything we have learned throughout the past nine chapters. You can consider this as a 'cheat sheet' to have an easy access for all the essential information about our beloved cat.

Persian Cat 101

Origin: Iran (Persia)

Breed Size: big size

Body Type and Appearance: It has a short body, with thick legs and a short neck. Also, its tail is short and small ears. The head is rounded with large rounded eyes.

Height: 10 -1 5 inches for male, 10 – 14 inches for female

Weight: less than 12 lbs for Male, and eight to 12 lbs for Female

Coat Length: long

Coat Texture: silky

Color: red, black, chocolate, silver, cameo, blue-cream, calico, white, cream, blue, lilac, golden, tortoiseshell, brown, seal

Patterns: tortoiseshell, tricolor/calico, smoke, points, solid, bicolor, tabby, shaded

Temperament: elegant, gentle, graceful, kind, quiet, not particularly shy, need human companionship,

Strangers: not that friendly around strangers

Other Cats: gets along well with other cat

Other Pets: may get along well with other pets if properly socialized, may chase small pets

With Children: Not that great with children, unless the child is gentle and won't cause the cat anxiety.

Exercise Needs: needs daily exercise through running or walking around a fenced yard

Social Needs: Moderate

Health Conditions: this breed develops hereditary health issues. The issues include progressive retinal atrophy (PRA), bladder stones, liver shunts, polycystic kidney disease (PKD), hypertrophic cardiomyopathy (HCM), cystitis (bladder infection)

Lifespan: average 8 to 11 years

Legal Requirements and Cat Licensing:

United States: The country has no federal requirement for licensing cat, however, some states have their own rules.

United Kingdom and Other Countries: You need to obtain special special permit if you want to travel with your pet abroad. Locate the country that you want to fly to and check the specific requirements for them.

Purchasing and Selecting a Healthy Breed

Where to Purchase: Cat conventions, backyard breeders, online sellers, and etc.

Characteristics of a Reputable Breeder: We have given you a lot information about this reputable breeder. However, the best way to know if the breeder is a reputable one is to carefully inspect the place of their business. Look at the litter and figure out if they are happy or not. Other than that, a reputable breeder will ask you questions about yourself, this is because the breeder might want to know where the cat might end up.

Characteristics of a Healthy Breed: You need to carefully inspect the cat. You need to come close and personal to the cat to make sure there are no defects or sickness to it.

Habitat Requirements for Persian Cats: You need to provide an adequate space for your cat. It needs to have its own space for the scratching post, food and water bowl, and the litter box.

Housing Temperature: the normal house temperature should be just right, not too cold nor too hot.

Nutrition and Food

How to Feed Your Cat: There are three methods in which you can feed your cat. You can do a trial and error method to figure out what is best for your cat. You can also ask your vet for his or her recommendation on what is the best method for your cat.

Feeding Amount/Frequency: Amount and frequency of food intake depends on the age, size, and energy level of your kitten or cat. Make sure you coordinate with your vet to know more.

Persian Cat's Grooming

How to Brush Your Cat's Teeth: Start slow and accustom your cat into having its teeth brush. Do it once a week until you can do it weekend.

How to Trim Your Cat's Nails: Practice this habit of cutting the nails. Trim the nails once a month until it can accustom to be cut once a week.

Cleaning Your Cat's Ears: Remove the normal wax build - up using a cat ear cleaning solution and squeeze a few drops in the ear canal. However, you just do this occasionally.

Breeding Your Persian Cats

Gestation Period: 65 to 67 days or around 6 weeks

Litter Size: Persian cats typically give birth to 6 kittens on average and up to a maximum of 12 kittens

Maturity: They become fully mature at around five years

Recommended Vaccinations:

- ✓ Panleukopenia
- ✓ Rabies
- ✓ Feline Leukemia
- ✓ Chlamydophila
- ✓ Feline Infectious Peritonitis
- ✓ Bordetella
- ✓ Giardia
- ✓ Feline Immunodeficiency Virus
- ✓ Rhinotracheitis
- ✓ Calicivirus

Glossary of Cat Terms

Abundism – Referring to a cat that has markings more prolific than is normal.

Acariasis – A type of mite infection.

ACF – Australian Cat Federation

Affix – A cattery name that follows the cat's registered name; cattery owner, not the breeder of the cat.

Agouti – A type of natural coloring pattern in which individual hairs have bands of light and dark coloring.

Ailurophile – A person who loves cats.

Albino – A type of genetic mutation which results in little to no pigmentation, in the eyes, skin, and coat.

Allbreed – Referring to a show that accepts all breeds or a judge who is qualified to judge all breeds.

Alley Cat – A non-pedigreed cat.

Alter – A desexed cat; a male cat that has been neutered or a female that has been spayed.

Amino Acid – The building blocks of protein; there are 22 types for cats, 11 of which can be synthesized and 11 which must come from the diet (see essential amino acid).

Anestrus – The period between estrus cycles in a female cat.

Any Other Variety (AOV) – A registered cat that doesn't conform to the breed standard.

ASH – American Shorthair, a breed of cat.

Back Cross – A type of breeding in which the offspring is mated back to the parent.

Balance – Referring to the cat's structure; proportional in accordance with the breed standard.

Barring – Describing the tabby's striped markings.

Base Color – The color of the coat.

Bicolor – A cat with patched color and white.

Blaze – A white coloring on the face, usually in the shape of an inverted V.

Bloodline – The pedigree of the cat.

Brindle – A type of coloring, a brownish or tawny coat with streaks of another color.

Castration – The surgical removal of a male cat's testicles.

Cat Show – An event where cats are shown and judged.

Cattery – A registered cat breeder; also, a place where cats may be boarded.

CFA – The Cat Fanciers Association.

Cobby – A compact body type.

Colony – A group of cats living wild outside.

Color Point – A type of coat pattern that is controlled by color point alleles; pigmentation on the tail, legs, face, and ears with an ivory or white coat.

Colostrum – The first milk produced by a lactating female; contains vital nutrients and antibodies.

Conformation – The degree to which a pedigreed cat adheres to the breed standard.

Cross Breed – The offspring produced by mating two distinct breeds.

Dam – The female parent.

Declawing – The surgical removal of the cat's claw and first toe joint.

Developed Breed – A breed that was developed through selective breeding and crossing with established breeds.

Down Hairs – The short, fine hairs closest to the body which keep the cat warm.

DSH – Domestic Shorthair.

Estrus – The reproductive cycle in female cats during which she becomes fertile and receptive to mating.

Fading Kitten Syndrome – Kittens that die within the first two weeks after birth; the cause is generally unknown.

Feral – A wild, untamed cat of domestic descent.

Gestation – Pregnancy; the period during which the fetuses develop in the female's uterus.

Guard Hairs – Coarse, outer hairs on the coat.

Harlequin – A type of coloring in which there are van markings of any color with the addition of small patches of the same color on the legs and body.

Inbreeding – The breeding of related cats within a closed group or breed.

Kibble – Another name for dry cat food.

Lilac – A type of coat color that is pale pinkish-gray.

Line – The pedigree of ancestors; family tree.

Litter – The name given to a group of kittens born at the same time from a single female.

Mask – A type of coloring seen on the face in some breeds.

Matts – Knots or tangles in the cat's fur.

Mittens – White markings on the feet of a cat.

Moggie – Another name for a mixed breed cat.

Mutation – A change in the DNA of a cell.

Muzzle – The nose and jaws of an animal.

Natural Breed – A breed that developed without selective breeding or the assistance of humans.

Neutering – Desexing a male cat.

Open Show – A show in which spectators are allowed to view the judging.

Pads – The thick skin on the bottom of the feet.

Particolor – A type of coloration in which there are markings of two or more distinct colors.

Patched – A type of coloration in which there is any solid color, tabby, or tortoiseshell color plus white.

Pedigree – A purebred cat; the cat's papers showing its family history.

Pet Quality – A cat that is not deemed of high enough standard to be shown or bred.

Piebald – A cat with white patches of fur.

Points – Also color points; markings of contrasting color on the face, ears, legs, and tail.

Pricked – Referring to ears that sit upright.

Purebred – A pedigreed cat.

Queen – An intact female cat.

Roman Nose – A type of nose shape with a bump or arch.

Scruff – The loose skin on the back of a cat's neck.

Selective Breeding – A method of modifying or improving a breed by choosing cats with desirable traits.

Senior – A cat that is more than 5 but less than 7 years old.

Sire – The male parent of a cat.

Solid – Also self; a cat with a single coat color.

Spay – Desexing a female cat.

Stud – An intact male cat.

Tabby – A type of coat pattern consisting of a contrasting color over a ground color.

Tom Cat – An intact male cat.

Tortoiseshell – A type of coat pattern consisting of a mosaic of red or cream and another base color.

Tri-Color – A type of coat pattern consisting of three distinct colors in the coat.

Tuxedo – A black and white cat.

Unaltered – A cat that has not been desexed.

Index

A

amino acid 108
antibodies 110

B

body 110, 111
breed 109, 110, 111, 112, 113
breeder 108, 109
breeding 109, 110, 111, 112

C

Cat Fanciers Association 110
cattery 108
CFA 110
claw 110
coat 108, 109, 110, 111, 113
color 109, 110, 111, 112, 113
cycle 111

D

desexed 108, 113
diet 108
DNA 112
domestic 111

E

ears 110, 112
essential 108

estrus 109

F

face 109, 110, 111, 112
family 111, 112
feet 111, 112
female 108, 109, 110, 111, 113
fertile 111
food 111
fur 111, 112

G

genetic 108

I

infection 108
intact 113

J

judge 108

K

kittens 111

L

lactating 110

M

male	108, 109, 112, 113
markings	108, 109, 111, 112
milk	110
mite	108
mutation	108

N

neutered	108
nose	112, 113
nutrients	110

O

offspring	109, 110

P

pattern	108, 110, 113
pedigree	109, 111
pets	
pigmentation	108, 110
protein	108
purebred	112

S

show	108, 112
skin	108, 112, 113
standard	109, 110, 112

T

tail 110, 112

traits 113

Photo Credits

Page 1 Photo by user Arash Razzagh Karimi via Flickr.com, https://www.flickr.com/photos/arash_rk/3764944874/

Page 4 Photo by user Franco Vannini via Flickr.com, https://www.flickr.com/photos/25168691@N06/15404884070/

Page 16 Photo by user Magnus Bråth via Flickr.com, https://www.flickr.com/photos/magnusbrath/5339239144/

Page 30 Photo by user Ashley Bayles via Flickr.com, https://www.flickr.com/photos/ashleybayles/9571304225/

Page 40 Photo by user Paul Sullivan via Flickr.com, https://www.flickr.com/photos/pfsullivan_1056/8729452606/

Page 51 Photo by user kitty.green66 via Flickr.com, https://www.flickr.com/photos/53887959@N07/4985430014/

Page 60 Photo by user kitty.green66 via Flickr.com, https://www.flickr.com/photos/53887959@N07/4984831661/

Page 66 Photo by user Magnus Bråth via Flickr.com, https://www.flickr.com/photos/magnusbrath/5391136326/

Page 76 Photo by user djembar lembasono via Flickr.com, https://www.flickr.com/photos/donjirori/202475929/

Page 89 Photo by user Brad via Flickr.com, https://www.flickr.com/photos/bfra07/5652581247/

Page 101 Photo by user Shawn Harquail via Flickr.com, https://www.flickr.com/photos/harquail/17307930963/

References

"Persian" – The International Cat Association

https://www.tica.org/en/cat-breeds/item/249-persian-introduction

"Persian Cat Information and Personality Traits" - Hillspet.com

https://www.hillspet.com/cat-care/cat-breeds/persian

"Persian" – Vetstreet.com

http://www.vetstreet.com/cats/persian#1_ugw20zmq

"Persian History, Part 1" - Persianbc.org

https://www.persianbc.org/history1.php

"About Persian Cats" – Catsofpersia.com

https://www.catsofpersia.com/first-persian-cat/

"Travelling with your cat" – IcatCare.org

https://icatcare.org/advice/travelling-with-your-cat

"12 Essential Kitten Supplies Every Pet Owner Needs" - Bandofcats.com

http://www.bandofcats.com/essential-kitten-supplies/

"Persian Cat Breed" - Petwave.com

https://www.petwave.com/Cats/Breeds/Persian.aspx

"Persian Cat Adoption - Pros and Cons" – Persiancatsblog.blogspot.com

http://persiancatsblog.blogspot.com/2010/11/persian-cat-adoption-pros-and-cons.html

"Legal requirements for cat owners" – Victoria State Government

http://agriculture.vic.gov.au/pets/cats/legal-requirements-for-cat-owners

"Legal and social responsibilities of owning a pet" - Petpep.ava.com.au

http://petpep.ava.com.au/pets_legal_responsibilities

"Cat or Kitten: Which Should You Adopt?" - Meowcatrescue.org

http://www.meowcatrescue.org/resources/articles/15/cat-or-kitten-which-should-you-adopt/index.html

"Considerations Prior to Buying a Cat or Kitten" – Petwebsite.co.uk

http://www.petwebsite.co.uk/cats/buying-a-cat/considerations-prior-to-buying-a-cat

"How To Select A Responsible Cat Breeder" - Pets4homes.co.uk

https://www.pets4homes.co.uk/pet-advice/how-to-select-a-responsible-cat-breeder.html

"10 Tips to Keep Your Cat Happy Indoors" - Humanesociety.org

http://www.humanesociety.org/animals/cats/tips/cat_happy_indoors.html

"Meal Feeding vs. Free Feeding Cats: What's Best?" - Hillspet.com

https://www.hillspet.com/cat-care/nutrition-feeding/how-to-feed-a-cat

"What to Know About Feeding Your Cat" – WebMD.com

https://pets.webmd.com/cats/guide/cat-food-101-what-you-need-to-know-about-feeding-your-cat#1

"Foods that are Dangerous or Toxic to Cats" – Hillspet.com

https://www.hillspet.com/cat-care/nutrition-feeding/toxic-foods-for-cats

"Cat Grooming Basics" - Vetbabble.com

https://www.vetbabble.com/cats/grooming-cats/grooming-tips/

"Cat Grooming Tips" - ASPCA.org

https://www.aspca.org/pet-care/cat-care/cat-grooming-tips

"Persian Official Breed Standard" – Cat Fanciers Organization

http://cfa.org/Portals/0/documents/breeds/standards/persian.pdf

"HOW TO TRAIN A CAT FOR A SHOW" – MOM.ME

http://animals.mom.me/how-to-train-a-cat-for-a-show-12112470.html

"Kitten Training for Show" – PurrInLot.com

https://www.purrinlot.com/kitten-training-show.htm

"Cat Breeding" – Petwave.com

https://www.petwave.com/Cats/Basics/Breeding.aspx

"Most Common Health Problems in Persian Cats" – Knoji.com

https://pets.knoji.com/most-common-health-problems-in-persian-cats/

"Kitten Proofing Your Home with 10 Easy-to-Follow Tips" – Hillspet.com

https://www.hillspet.com/cat-care/training/tips-for-kitten-proofing-your-home

www.ingramcontent.com/pod-product-compliance
Lightning Source LLC
Chambersburg PA
CBHW060838050426
42453CB00008B/743